Table of Contents

What is the purpose of boundaries?

Today's Scriptures
·Proverbs 8: 29
·Job 38: 8-11
·Psalm 104: 5-9

The sea is often described as chaos in the Bible. It is something that cannot be contained or tamed. It is a monstrous beast that will overtake people quickly if you don't have a large boat, and sometimes can even when you do. In this verse we see that God gave the sea a boundary so that the waters could not cross over to land.

We see three reasons or purposes for boundaries in these verses.

1. He is protecting us. Job 38: 8-11 & Exodus 19:12. God put limits for Mount Sinai. The people were not to touch the mountain or they would be put to death.
2. He is protecting His property. Genesis 1:29-31, Genesis 2:8-17, Genesis 3: 21-24. The command is do not eat and the consequence is that we will die if we do eat.
3. He is protecting Himself. He did not want to see us suffer for an eternity by eating from the tree of life so he had to ban us from the garden.

The boundaries we set should follow these guidelines given to us by God

1. Protect ourselves
2. Protect our property
3. Protect others

Personal Reflection

When has God or someone you know given you a boundary?

How did it make you feel?

How did you react to your boundary?

Characteristics of Healthy Boundaries

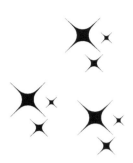

- Boundaries must come from a healed, not hurting heart.
- They are not about controlling others.
- They are about putting limits on what you will or will not accept.
- It's not about punishment, but about consequences.

CHARACTERISTICS OF UNHEALTHY BOUNDARIES

- Desire for control
- Fear of rejection
- Lack of experience

GOD SET BOUNDARIES FOR US AND THE WORLD HE CREATED

- Proverbs 8: 29
- Job 38: 10
- Exodus 19: 12
- Psalm 104: 9
- Genesis 3: 21-24
- Genesis 2: 8-17

Verse 16: you are free to eat from any tree of the garden; but you must not eat from the tree of knowledge of good and evil, for when you eat from it you will certainly die.

This verse shows a good structure for a boundary
1.Give a freedom
2.State a restriction
State a consequence for violating that restriction

Examples

- When you get home from school you are free to have any snack you want, but you can only have one. If you have more than one, then you will not get dessert after dinner.
- It really affects my mood negatively when you talk negatively about our finances. When we talk about finances, I would like it if you could be positive, upbeat, and ready for solutions. If you choose to speak negatively, I will choose to end the conversation until you can speak positively again.

Personal Reflection

Have you set an unhealthy boundary with someone?

How can you re-write that boundary for it to be healthy?

Practice saying this out loud several times before bringing it up to the person.

Boundary Stones

Today's Verses:
·Job 24: 2
·Proverbs 23: 10
·Proverbs 22: 28
·Hosea 5: 10
·Deuteronomy 27: 17
·Psalm 16: 6

Before GPS, surveys, and property lines, the ancient peoples used stones to mark their property lines. If a neighbor wanted more land, they wouldn't pick the stone up and move it several feet. The other property owner would be more likely to notice a large movement. Instead, they would slowly move it, a little bit at a time until they had gained more property for themselves at such a slow pace, their neighbor hadn't even recognized the stones had been moved!

Our personal boundaries are very similar to this. If people make a huge violation, it's obvious. We would immediately confront the situation or cut ties with the person. It's the smaller violations that are harder to recognize. Little by little, a person can violate our boundaries without us recognizing these violations until we are accepting behavior from them we would have never tolerated before.

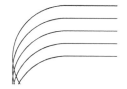

When we recognize that our boundaries have been violated we should first stop and talk with God about it. Tell Him that you have seen that you have let your boundaries be violated by not noticing these little things over time. Ask Him to forgive you for not noticing. Ask Him to give you wisdom about how to move forward. How you can reestablish your boundary with that person.

Personal Reflection

Is there someone who has slowly encroached on your boundaries?

What happened?

How did you get to where you are right now with them?

How did you contribute to the problem?

Ask God to give you wisdom and discernment for reestablishing healthy boundaries.

Conflict Resolution

Today's Verse: Matthew 18: 15-20

These verses give an excellent framework for handling conflict.

1. Go to the person who has sinned against you and talk with them
2. If nothing changes, or no agreement is met, go to them again with 1 or 2 more people.
3. If nothing changes, or no agreement is met, tell it to the church
4. If they still don't listen, treat them as you would a pagan or tax collector

A while back, I was going through a difficult time with a friend. I met with a spiritual mentor and asked if there was a Biblical framework for dealing with conflict. The mentor pointed me to these verses.

In difficult situations, it is often tempting to go talk to everyone else but the person who has sinned against you. Maybe it's a need to share our pain with others or maybe it's conflict avoidance, but these verses make it clear that we should first confront them face to face, just the two of us.

Clear the air. Tell them how they have sinned against you and how it has made you feel, and judge their reaction. If they apologize and ask how they can fix the situation, then you're free to move on without telling others about the problem. If, however, they refuse to accept responsibility for their actions, then it's time to get one or two others (strong Christians I might add) to go with you to talk to them again.

These people you take with you can act as advisors and negotiators. They can listen to the other person's side of the story and help you see if you have done anything wrong in this process as well. This is why it's important for these people to be strong Christians who have similar morals and life views.

If this person still refuses to listen, it says to bring it to the Church. I don't think this means to get up in front of the Church and tell everyone your story. I think this means that the two of you should try to meet with church leadership to present the issues and get Biblical guidance from a strong Christian in leadership.

If they refuse to listen even to the Church, then it says to treat them as you would a pagan or tax collector. Tax collectors were viewed as unethical, hated, and regarded as sinners.

If someone is inside the church (a Christian) and acting in a sinful manner, then we should not associate with them any longer because this would give a bad name to Christians. This is called righteous judgement. We are allowed to judge those within the church. The sinners outside the church we are called to love because our hope is that in loving them, we win them to Christ to change the way they are living.

Tomorrow we will take a look at a few types of people we are told not to associate with.

Personal Reflection

Do you have conflict with someone at the moment?

Have you spoken with them about it face to face, just the two of you?

Why or why not?

If not, are you willing to do this?

Who We Shouldn't Associate With

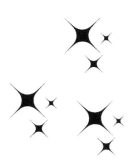

TODAY'S VERSES

- Proverbs 19:19
- Matthew 7:6
- 1 Corinthians 5:11
- Proverbs 15:25
- Exodus 23:32

DESCRIPTORS OF THOSE WE SHOULD NOT ASSOCIATE WITH

- Angry
- Unholy
- Proud
- People who worship idols
- Believers who participate in sexual sin
- Greedy
- Abusive
- Drunkards
- Cheats people

Have you heard the saying "you become the average of the five people you spend the most time with?" The people you surround yourself with have an influence on your thoughts, emotions, and behaviors in both positive and negative ways.

If you have kids, you have probably seen this in either your child or a friend's child. You have a good kid, making good grades, but somehow, they get in with the wrong crowd and start skipping school, making bad grades, partying all the time, and over time become unrecognizable from the person they used to be.

In recovery, patients are statistically more likely to relapse if they go back to the same environment with the same friends who were using with them before treatment. Creating an environment of people who believe in the person's ability to recover, who offer hope, support, and encouragement, is an important factor in the recovery process.

It's also extremely important for us in everyday life. If you surround yourself with women who are constantly complaining, you will soon find yourself complaining right along with them. We want to surround ourselves with people who most exemplify the person we want to become.

PERSONAL REFLECTION

Are you a good influence on the people you hang around with?

Are your friends positive influences, or is it time to look for new ones?

If you find yourself needing to make new friends, it's a good idea to determine what you want in your life so that you can look for friends who have those things. Their influence on you can help you obtain those things. What traits do you want your new friends to have?

Expanding Your Borders

TODAY'S VERSES

- Isaiah 26:15
- Isaiah 54: 2-8
- Exodus 23:3
- Micah 7:11

Boundaries are meant to protect our hearts, the source of our emotions, from the actions of others. Think of it like building a wall around your heart to keep the arrows of the enemy's bow from hitting you directly. The hope is that the arrows will hit the wall and your heart will be protected.

This is great for us when we are just beginning to heal. It helps protect us from the unknown and gives us a safe place to heal and grow stronger. In Exodus 23:30, we see God tell Israel that He will drive the enemy out a little at a time until the population has increased enough to take possession of the land.

Inside the protective walls of our boundaries, we will heal and grow in strength until we are strong enough to expand our borders. This is the ultimate goal, to expand our borders. Jesus doesn't want us staying in a tiny fenced-in area. He wants us to grow and expand in strength.

We can expand our borders in two ways:
1. We grow and learn to process other's behaviors or
2. Other people's behaviors improve because of the boundaries we have set and they show us they are worthy of more trust and responsibility.

Let's talk about #1 today. In keeping with the arrow metaphor, think of a person's actions being an arrow they are shooting at you. In the beginning of this journey, each arrow may feel like it is aimed directly at your heart, and every time one hits you, it is super painful. It feels like you might just die. As you heal from trauma and past negative experiences, you learn that other people's behavior is snot about you. It's about them, and their needs, or their lack of knowing God. When they launch an arrow at you, you now have a shield in your hand. You can knock the arrows away. They no longer hit you. Their behavior no longer affects you negatively. When they do something that used to really hurt you, you find yourself being unaffected. You might say, that's just who they are. That action is about their unhealed emotions or pain. It's not about me.

When this happens, you know you have been strengthened enough to expand your borders. That doesn't mean you automatically give this person full access to your life. Just expand a little bit at a time.

PERSONAL REFLECTION

Do you have any areas of your life where you previously had walls, but now feel like you are equipped with a shield?

What's different now about how you feel in these areas?

How did you grow in strength in these areas?

Jesus Meets His Personal Needs

Jesus had no problem meeting his personal needs. You never see anywhere in the Bible that Jesus burned out and quit his ministry. Read today's verses to see how Jesus met His personal needs.

·Rest: Mark 4:38. Jesus slept and rested on the boat. Obviously, no one else was sleeping here. He knew He needed rest and took a nap.
·Time Alone: Luke 5:15-16. Jesus often withdrew to solitude.
·Let Others Serve Him: Luke 7: 36-38, John 10: 39-42, John 12: 2-3.

Self-care is the process of establishing behaviors to ensure holistic well-being of oneself, to promote health, and actively manage illness when it occurs. Examples of self-care are getting enough sleep, eating healthy foods, spending time with loved ones, and spending time alone with God. In today's verses, we see Jesus doing all these things.

The root to self-care is boundaries. It's saying no to something to say yes to your own emotional, physical, and mental well-being. Up until this point, you may have only been thinking about very specific boundaries with specific people, but boundaries can be general, overall guidelines as well.

These general guidelines can be extremely helpful for preventing bad relationships from moving past the initial get to know you phase.

For instance, let's say you are dating, and one of your boundaries is: I will be respected by my significant other. If on a date, your dating partner is pushing you to be physical after you have told them you do not want to be physical until marriage, then you can more easily recognize that your boundary is being crossed and can end the relationship before it goes any further.

Personal Reflection

What general boundaries do you need to establish in your life? (Think about relationships, work, time management, health, etc.)

How do these support your mental, emotional, or physical health?

What might be some warning signs that someone is violating these boundaries?

Jesus Says No to Inappropriate Behavior

Jesus has no problem telling people like it is. He is honest, upfront, and kind but also stern. He doesn't typically beat around the bush or play games. As you read today's verses, look for how Jesus is saying no to these inappropriate behaviors.

- Abuse: Luke 4: 28-30. An angry mob was going to push Him off a cliff, but he passed right through the crowd and went on his way. He didn't use any words, he didn't fight back, he didn't defend himself, he just walked right through them.
- Entitlement: Matthew 12: 46-50. Jesus said that just because they were his mother and brother, didn't mean they got special access to him. Everyone who follows God is his relative.
- Baiting Questions: Matthew 21: 23-27. Learn to recognize when someone is asking a sincere question vs. a question that might entrap us. He didn't point this out to them, instead, he asked a question back to them. Matthew 22: 15-22. This time he does point out that they are trying to entrap him, but he still asks a question in return. He has discernment to know they are trying to trick him.

- Cynicism: Luke 23: 8-9. Jesus refused to answer Herod's questions because He was filled with cynicism. This reminds me of the phrase: 'there's no arguing with stupid.' If someone isn't willing to listen, then why talk?
- Manipulation: Matthew 16: 22-23. Peter was trying to manipulate Jesus out of following God's plan for his life. His actions were well-meaning, but he did not consult God before doing it so he had no idea if he was acting on the authority of God or not. He was simply trying to talk Jesus out of it because he didn't want to lose him.
- Pride: Matthew 13:54-58. The people were full of pride, and because of this, Jesus only did a few miracles in his hometown.

Discernment: to understand or know something through the power of the Spirit. It includes perceiving the true character of people and the source and meaning of spiritual manifestations.

Wisdom: Bible-based, Christ-centered, and Spirit-led knowledge. It seeks to glorify the Lord and not oneself, by focusing on the eternal sagacity of Jesus' atoning sacrifice. Can be human wisdom, demonic wisdom, or Godly wisdom.

How do we grow in discernment or wisdom?
1. Fear God Proverbs 9:10
2. Desire Wisdom & Discernment Proverbs 2:4
3. Pray for Wisdom & Discernment James 1:5
4. Study God's word Psalm 19:7

PERSONAL REFLECTION

Do you have a situation in the past couple of weeks that felt off?

Looking back, was the person using one of these tactics?

What are some signs you can recognize the next time this happens? This may be what you were thinking or feeling when the situation was happening.

Speak Truth in Love

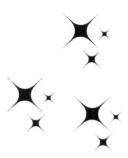

As you read today's verses, ask yourself if you would be able to say the things Jesus does if you were in the same situation.

Today's Verses:
- Matthew 21: 12-17
- John 2: 12-16
- Matthew 19: 13-21

I recently watched a TV show where there was a group of people who practiced radical honesty. They spoke the truth no matter what, regardless of how it would make other people feel. When they started this practice, at first it felt freeing. It was great to say what you were thinking without filtering it. It felt good to not have to come up with white lies to protect others. Soon, other people in their lives were not liking these people. The things they would say were harsh, unkind, and sometimes downright rude.

The thing I noticed as I watched this is that although we do need to speak the truth, it can't always be so direct and without any thought to how it might affect the other person. When what we need to say has the potential to hurt someone we need to temper it with lots of love.

Unfortunately, for those of us who have problems with boundaries, we often take this to the extreme. Our need to please people and our discomfort with confrontation keeps us from saying what needs to be said. We notice things that are wrong. We should speak up, but we don't want to hurt their feelings, so we keep quiet, enduring the bad behavior from the other person. As each situation comes and goes without being addressed, we become passive.

As you read the above verses, you likely noticed that Jesus is not passive. He is full of passion and zeal. He is not afraid to say what needs to be said. He's not afraid to tell people they are wrong. He's not scared to point out wrong beliefs and bad behaviors. He's not troubled by going against the mainstream way of doing things. Proverbs 27: 17 says 'As iron sharpens iron, so a friend sharpens a friend.' It is our duty as believers to help other believers grow in their faith and become more like Jesus. We cannot fulfill this calling if we remain passive. Passion, zeal, and speaking truth in love are a requirement!

PERSONAL REFLECTION

Have you become passive in your relationships?

Are you open to correction from your friends?

What's one, simple way you can begin speaking truth in love to others today?

Jesus Brings The Peace

Today's Verse:
·John 8:1-11

Jesus was preaching when the Pharisees brought the woman in to accuse her. I don't know about you, but I would be highly annoyed if someone interrupted me mid-sentence. However, Jesus remained calm.

Verse 6 says He knew they were trying to trap Him, so He did not respond. Instead, He knelt down and began drawing in the sand. Now, I know that Jesus is very wise, and He may have already known His answer, but what if His kneeling and doodling in the sand actually gave Him time to think. He did not respond rashly and without thought just because they were demanding an answer.

When He does respond, he did not answer their question. As we have seen in our previous verses, his M.O. is not to answer questions that will entrap Him. He essentially asks who here is without sin? Then goes back to doodling.

I would love to have this calm composure in the chaos of life. There's also an air of confidence that He knows without a doubt that He is right. He is not doubting, complaining, or mistrusting His own interpretation of the circumstances the Pharisees keep putting Him in.

The thought model describes what happens when we have thoughts about our circumstances. First, we have the thought, which is a judgement about the circumstance, that thought creates an emotion, that emotion produces or drives our action, and then we get a result.

PERSONAL REFLECTION

Peace can be the emotion or the result. In a difficult circumstance in your life, what can you think to feel peace?

What can you think, feel, and do to create peace?

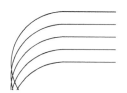

Where Is Your Reality?

TODAY'S VERSES

- Colossians 3:1-2
- Isaiah 26: 3
- Philippians 4: 8
- Romans 2: 2
- Isaiah 55: 8-9
- Romans 12: 2
- Proverbs 16: 20
- 2 Corinthians 10: 5
- Proverbs 18:21
- Isaiah 26:3

Have you heard the saying 'My perspective is my reality'? While this is somewhat true, the danger in this statement is that our thoughts create our reality, so if our thoughts are not focused on God, then our reality, or our perspective, can be skewed.

If our thoughts aren't focused on God, then what are they focused on? Typically, the opposite of God's thoughts would be the lies of the enemy and the enemy hates relationships, so his thoughts are always going to try to undermine relationships in our lives.

The Bible says to guard your heart for it is the well spring of life. How do we guard our heart (emotions)? We guard our hear by directing our thoughts to God's thoughts so that we are creating healthy emotions.

The heart is the wellspring of life because our emotions drive our actions, and our actions are what create the results in our lives.

Let's give a simplified example. Let's say you think someone doesn't like you. When you get around this person, you likely act much different than you do with a friend. You probably don't talk as much. Why? Because you probably feel fear that they are judging you. You don't act like your true self. You may be short with them and provide curt answers to any questions.

Now, think about if you were on the receiving end of this behavior. How would you feel about this person? You might feel like they are phony or withholding information. If you feel like that, then you may begin to not like them or want to be around them.

Essentially, you have provided behavior that reinforces your thoughts that this person doesn't like you. You have created your reality.

If instead, we can begin to focus our thoughts on God's thoughts, we can begin to create better relationships in our lives.

PERSONAL REFLECTION

What are some common thoughts you have that are more aligned with the lies of the enemy that the truth of God?

What does the Bible say is the truth in these areas?

GREETINGS FROM

MISTY KNIGHT &
TENACIOUS WOMAN MINISTRIES

As we conclude our Bible Study on boundaries, we extend heartfelt thanks for journeying with us. Your commitment to exploring the depths of God's Word is truly appreciated. Our earnest desire is that, through these pages, you not only gained insights into setting boundaries but also grew intimately acquainted with the character of God. May this understanding guide you in cultivating healthy boundaries and drawing nearer to His grace. For further resources and community support, visit www.tenaciouswomanministries.org.

Milton Keynes UK
Ingram Content Group UK Ltd.
UKHW050636130224
437765UK00013B/450